AF413709

Come Sit With Me for a Moment

FRANK BAILLARGEON

COME SIT WITH ME FOR A MOMENT

A TIMELESS COLLECTION OF POETRY, IMPRESSIONS, & LYRICS

COME SIT WITH ME FOR A MOMENT

Cover Art by Annelise Joy Farquhar

Book and Cover Design by Stacey Smekofske @ EditsbyStacey.com

Published by Frank Writes History

Identifiers

Digital: 979-8-9866040-6-0

Paperback: 979-8-9866040-7-7

Hardcover: 979-8-9866040-8-4

FRANK WRITES

HISTORY

For my Family

Contents

Merry Christmas

A chilly Christmas has arrived.
It seems a lifetime since our last.
We'd spent a dozen years or more
Never feeling winter's blast.

"How could this have happened?" I ask,
    blowing on my hands.
Why, we should be out walking
On Coronado's Silver Strand.

It's good to make the best of things.
We've bought our winter gear.
We even plan on staying here
For at least another year.

But, really, there's a limit
To the goodwill one can muster.
When wrapped up like two sausages
Braving Old Man Winter's bluster.

Boise's a fine place, no doubt.
In so many ways, a treasure.
But, darn it, we can't figure out
How to overcome this weather!

Well, Love, here's my plan
To survive the winter season.
I promise to seek you out each hour for
      no apparent reason.

And place my arms around your neck
      until we stir.
At which point, we'll not likely hear
The sound of each other's "brrrrrrr."

Frank Baillargeon - 1995

Family Christmas in Boise

The big yellow house in wreaths and white lights -
You claim it looks perfect by day and by night.
You've filled it again with great childhood glee.
It's Santa Claus-ready, except for the tree.

How did it happen that we find ourselves here?
What Fates wove their magic to bring us this cheer.
We could be in Boston or Detroit, or crimminy,
Warming ourselves by an Arkansas chimney.

But, no, we are cheerily spending the season
In the warmth of our dear home, whatever the reason.
In just a short while, that home will be glad
For the giddy arrival of Frank, Beth, and Chad.

In their wake, we will welcome their spouses and more.
We will welcome our grandkids, one, two, three and four.
Todd and Stacy will wonder in earnest dismay
At the silly traditions and flashy displays.

We'll feed them all goodies and food from their past.
We'll watch Christmas movies and leave all aghast
As we roll out the photos and movies that show
Three now grown-up children a long time ago.

Sierra and Andrue and Quentin and Anna
Will curl up to listen to stories from Nana.
Santa, and Frosty, and Rudolph and trains
Will crowd out all thoughts in their little kid brains.

Now, Christmas Eve finds us adorning the tree.
It's loaded with treasures but quite tinsel-free.
We'll sing Christmas jingles with reckless delight
While gorging on pepperoni bread through the night.

We'll argue for hours about the one thing
That we can or can't open after we sing.
It's finally settled for worse or for better
One gift will suffice, even a Grandma Gin sweater.

Papa reads us a story, a real Christmas smash,
Especially the part where we throw up the sash.
And now we're all ready to climb into bed
Was that the sound of the bells on his sled?

We'll lie there and giggle, unable to rest,
Tons of warm feelings well up in our chests.
We're gathered in Boise, a family complete,
Snuggled with loved ones, a holiday treat.
What magic, this moment, this rare interlude.

The stockings, the laughter, the kids, and the food.
We'll wake up tomorrow with new toys to play
And cherish forever this great Christmas day.

Frank Baillargeon - 1998

Home in Boise

For four years, we wandered far from our adopted Boise home. Work and family circumstances took us first to Michigan, then to San Francisco, then to northernmost California. Successful and necessary adventures all. Yet there remained a perpetual hole in our hearts.

Summer each year brought us back to celebrate the River Festival with our dear Idaho friends. Each time, we'd ache even more to return. Finally, last month, we came back.

More people have arrived here, which is startling. Amazing changes. Sprawling residential and commercial development. Big City traffic. Driving in via Oregon on a Saturday morning via 84 gave us our first moments of worry. Would we still recognize the Boise we cherished?

Our fear was unfounded. The character of our community thrives. Like a Dickens Ghost of Christmas Past, we wish we could take Boise residents to the places we've lived and worked. Only then could we accurately describe our joy and gratitude for being welcomed home.

Christmas is the perfect Boise holiday. It's the holiday that celebrates giving and brotherhood. We joined the thousands who braved the chilly weekend morning to kick off the season at the Holiday Parade. We wiped tears as the Color Guard marched by, and every man, woman, and child rose, with a hand over heart, and acknowledged our nation's flag. Our hearts were filled with joy watching young people passing candy to bundled children along the parade route.

We walked the streets of downtown, imagining each intersection as a potential Norman Rockwell masterpiece. At Saint Alphonsus Festival of Trees, we spent most of the day awed less by the magnificent trees than by the faces of our Boise neighbors, full of unguarded joy. We are ecstatic to see the legacy of "Somebody Needs You" continue, knowing that the community will eagerly help with any requests.

It's blissful to be home. To each of you whom we have passed in the supermarket, in the Post Office, and along our streets and greenbelt, thank you for sharing a smile. That does not happen in most other places. The willingness and silent commitment to acknowledge that we are all family and each loved marks the character of our community. Despite growth and change, that character is unchanged and unchanging.

Frank Baillargeon - 2003

Merry Christmas

SILENTLY

He stands transfixed beneath a clear December sky
Impossibly and boundlessly full of glittering objects
And he wonders, as his mind wanders
At the awesome splendor of it all.

HAPPILY

His breath traces its heavenward path
Only to disappear into the crisp night air,
Like the very thoughts that settle and depart
Absent his conscious beck and call.

PATIENTLY

He sets his collar against the bitter chill
To study that group of stars over there
Or that single brilliant planet just above
That could be the Christmas star, after all.

LOVINGLY

In these silent, happy, patient moments,
He knows that here, beneath this very sky,
Lie the connecting pieces of one perfect work of art.
Everyone he loves, the old and young, the near and far.

Frank Baillargeon - 2005

Behold

B ❄ Beyond all doubt,
Christmas draws out the best in us.

E ❄ Every year, we stop, consider those we
love and those who need, and we give.

H ❄ Happiness arrives in unexpected waves
from various origins–and prevails.

O ❄ Old Friends reach out, and new
acquaintances seal lasting new friendships.

L ❄ Love is everywhere, tugging at and
warming our collective hearts.

D ❄ Days are full of reverie and hope as
they hasten toward Christmas Day.

❄

U Under starry skies and festooned evergreens,
we discover ourselves in a new light.

N Nestled by the hearth, we recount and
refresh our memories and dreams.

T Together, we find forgiveness and renew
faith in family.

O Openly, we sing and laugh and cry tears of
tenderness and quiet yearning.

U Under the spell of Christmas, we become
children all, and miracles reign again.

S Shelter is ours from the harshest of our
instincts under the splendor of our
possibilities.

A All surrender to wonder and treasured
ritual – waiting.

C ❄ Christmas is our gift to one another of us
at our best.

H ❄ Holding forth for a moment each year
that we can all live in love.

I ❄ Inspired are we by the Child's story and
His Life.

L ❄ Living together in the season of Christmas,
as He would have us live each day.

D ❄ Devoid of anger, hatred, jealousy,
and despair. All gone. Perhaps forever.

❄

I ❄ In this splendid Christmas time, we look
deeper into others and ourselves.

S ❄ See not a stranger in the eyes of our
neighbor or within our soul.

❄

B ❄ Believing is easy when angels abound and
elves deliver treasures.

O ❄ Opening our hearts and minds to hear and
know our Truth.

R ❄ Reveling one and all in the joy and
knowledge that we are loved.

N ❄ No doubt this was what the Child intended.
Everyone. Every day. Everywhere.

Frank Baillargeon - 2006

It's Happened Again!

Before we got used to "two-thousand-and-seven"
A star stood above us, a greeting from heaven,
Inviting us all to share the delight
Of Christ's birthday revelry on this Christmas night.

(Santa even kissed Nana, now that was a sight!)

Before the year ended, we had the great pleasure
Of Heavilins arriving with Eli to treasure,
And Farquhar young ladies, a little bit tardy,
But arriving in time for our New Year's Eve Party.

(Or was it a 2ⁿᵈ Christmas Eve Party?)

Frank 3, and Isaac, with Nana and me,
Bring all to see their blooming forest and our humble tree.
Our houses are warm, and the treats are sure yummy.
It's easy to forget that the weather's quite crummy.

(Papa sure can rhyme things. He's not such a dummy!)

Christ had His birthday a few days ago,
And Santa scheduled two visits to Eagle, Idaho,
Though Papa was bold, way more often than wise,
And Isaac a little bit, too, once or twice.

(They should both have listened to Nana's advice!)

We love all the things that we do every year
As we gather once more in heartwarming cheer.
The songs that we butcher. The old movies we see.
Remind us how special a family can be.

(Copies of this can be bought for a fee!)

Frank Baillargeon - 2007

Even Though I'm Naughty

Dear Santa,

When I was a much younger boy,
and I could hardly wait,
I'd wake up and check the calendar
for that important date
When you arrive with presents
for good little girls and boys,
And I'd pray that I'd been good enough
for a couple of toys.

My parents always said
you saw me day and night.
I couldn't figure out how,
but my parents were always right.
So, every time I messed around
and wasn't very kind,
I hung my head and said a prayer

that, somehow, you wouldn't mind.

The years went by, and as they went,
I couldn't help but wonder
Why do you always bring me stuff
despite all my many blunders?
Now it's December once again,
and worry though I may,
This naughty boy knows Santa
comes on every Christmas Day.

Your friend,
Frankie

Frank Baillargeon - 2008

8 Christmas Gifts

PS3. Plastic tree. Bluetooth anything just for me.
A couple more toys for Josh and Kevin.

The Child would grow up to say:
"Blessed are the poor. Thiers is the Kingdom of Heaven."

Holiday cheer. Exotic beer. Texting loved ones far and near.
Things have gotten out of hand.

The Child would grow up to say:
"Blessed are the meek. They share possess the land."

Bigger. Flatter. Bursting carts. Megapixels off the chart. Electronic
wonders, all imported.

The Child would grow up to say:
"Blessed are they who mourn. They shall be comforted."

PC or MAC? Massage my poor back. Custom-tailored or off the
rack. Looking fine for all to see.

The Child would grow up to say:
"Blessed are the merciful. They shall obtain mercy."

Merry Christmas. Deck the Halls. Jingle Bells and chocolate balls.
Praying for a new iPod.

The Child would grow up to say:
"Blessed are the clean of heart. They shall see God."

Pray for Iraq or maybe Iran. Or is it now Afghanistan? Spoil the
child and spare the rod.

The Child would grow up to say:
"Blessed are the peacemakers.
They shall be called the children of God."

Behold, a Child was born this day.
In Bethlehem, so far away.
A King.
The Son of God, they say.
Appeared on that December Day.
In humble trappings,
He arrived and never to possessions strived.
And so, let's pause on this great morn
to embrace what He has given.

"Blessed are they that suffer persecution for justice' sake.
Theirs is the Kingdom of Heaven.

Frank Baillargeon - 2009

Up on Our Rooftop

Up on our rooftop, snowflakes fall,
Down comes good old Racoon Paul.
Down through the chimney with lots of noise,
That wakes all the good little girls and boys.

Yo-Yo-Yo. You should go.
Yo-Yo-Yo. You should go.
Up on the rooftop, slip, slip, slip.
Down on his bottom falls Old Saint Nick.

Off to the windows, we all fly,
Just in time to see Santa try
To climb up the trellis with lots of care,
Dragging a bag full of gifts to share.

Yo-Yo-Yo. We better go.
Yo-Yo-Yo. We better go.
Off to our beds now, quick, quick, quick,
Before Santa sees us and slips, slips, slips.

Just as you turn to rush off to bed,
A big loud crash fills us all with dread
Back at the window, we rush to see
The Big Guy hanging onto a tree.

Yo-Yo-Yo. We gotta go.
Yo-Yo-Yo. We gotta go.
Out to the front yard,
Quick as can be,
To help old Santa climb down that tree.

His face is all red now; embarrassed is he,
As we help get his big butt free.
He speaks not a word as he rubs his back.
Then, winks and hands us his big red sack.

Yo-Yo-Yo. Now we glow.
Yo-Yo-Yo. How we glow.
Out on the front lawn, tee-hee-hee,
Santa gave us gifts on Christmas Eve.

Frank Baillargeon - 2010

Knock Knock

Knock Knock

Who's there?"

"My name is Joseph. My wife, Mary, is with me. She's about to deliver our child."

"So?"

"We're wondering if you might have room for us tonight? It's freezing, and we're hungry and tired."

"Are you kidding? Please leave."

Knock Knock

"Who's there?"

"Joseph and Mary from Nazareth. We're about to deliver a baby. Can you provide us with some shelter?

"Sandy, there's a couple at our door. They want to spend the night. She looks like she's about to deliver a child. What should I do?"

"There's a fresh batch of cookies on the counter in the kitchen. Give them a few and send them on their way. They're probably just one of those homeless couples."

Knock Knock

"Who's there?"

"Santa."

"Please come in! Warm yourself over the fire. We've been anxiously awaiting you. Hey, everyone, Santa's here!"

How many doors would Joseph and Mary knock on today, knock, knock, before someone offered comfort, warmth, and compassion?

How many doors do each of us knock on before someone hears and welcomes us?

How many times have I heard knock knock and failed to answer?

I give thanks that Santa will bring me gifts this year and that I will give a gift or two to those I love. Santa is a symbol of the selfless love the Child would insist is the greatest of all virtues.

I give thanks for the times that I stood at a door, and that door (a home, a heart, a friendship, an opportunity) was thrown open. And my life was forever changed.

Christ isn't lost in our modern celebrations at Christmastime. He is there at every threshold.

Knock Knock

Frank Baillargeon - 2012

House of Memories

Memories are a special house
We build inside ourselves,
Where love and laughter linger,
Where all our past life dwells.

On holidays like Christmas,
We draw upon that store,
Reliving all our happy times,
And feeling that warmth once more

Wherever we may travel,
This house is always there,
To help to blend the old and new,
To build on, grow, and share.

This house can never get too full
Just grows from floor to floor,
Because the joy of memories
Is always making more.

My Christmas Eve at Target

It was Christmas Eve. I just waved
    goodbye to my very best friend.
We'd laughed through the night, fueled by
    sodas galore. A night without end.
Now Dad announced there are still things
    to buy.
"Come along," he insisted, though every
    trick did I try
To avoid the noise and the waiting and the
    traffic and worse.
But all my best efforts were wasted. I
    wanted to curse.

I slumped in the corner of our crummy
    backseat as Dad tried a shortcut in
    order to beat
The rush of humanity determined to
    spend their very last nickels on a gift
    or a treat.
My head just kept throbbing. Christmas
    music didn't help.

Dad was deaf to my agony. I wanted to
    yelp.
We sped round the corner past an empty
    tree market,
And screeched into the very last spot close
    to Target.

"Here's a few dollars," Dad said with a
    smile. "Go buy a soda. I'll be quite a
    while."
So, I watched him rush past the
    underwear racks and disappear as he
    turned at the discount backpacks.
Being no dummy, I stashed the cash and
    took off immediately to check out the
    toys.
From aisle to aisle, I wandered and tested
    every item for ten-year-old boys.
Hunger and thirst made a sudden return,
    so I headed up front with money in
    hand,
To check out the options at the crowded
    food stand.

With my stomach now bursting from the
    corn dog and Coke Free, I checked
    out the new PS3.
So off to the back of the Target, I went on
    a new mission, my money quite spent.
For hours I killed it on Ghost until,
    finally, I caved to the thing that I
    needed most.
Down past the hardware, I'd noticed
    before, was a stack of dog beds at the
    back of the store.

Up did I scramble over doggie breed
 themes, and in seconds was having
 some sugar plum dreams.
It might have been minutes, hours, or
 days when I woke with a start, my
 mind in a daze.

The silence was eerie. Not a person in
 sight. I leaped to the floor,
 overwhelmed with great fright.
I ran to the front of that Target so quickly
 that I collided head-on with my Dad,
 looking sickly.
We stood there a moment or two. Four
 eyes locked. Two hearts pounding.
Then we headed for home for my first
 Christmas grounding.

Frank Baillargeon - 2014

The Greatest Gift of All

Unto each girl and boy, at some age between seven and eleven,
There comes when fantasy gives way to floods of details.
A single overweight guy can't visit every house on Earth
in a single night.
Reindeer can't fly. Gifts don't come from elves
but from Cyber Monday sales.

Believing in magic is undeniably wondrous.
It's splendid to share the joy of innocence
in the face of Christmas lore,
To be a keeper of shared secrets
crafted from centuries of myth and custom
That will, sadly, devolve
into mundane and stealthy trips to the store.

On this Christmas, I saw myth's magic
grow into a far greater thing.
I watched as a young man discovered
an all-important truth about living.
No longer caring what presents awaited him
beneath a splendid tree.

Discovering, instead, that Christmas's true magic
and joy is in giving.

So, what did this young man choose to give
in this year of awakening?
Hugs to those in need. Food to comfort.
Time to share in traditions. Kindness.

I love Santa. I love holiday songs.
I love the giving and receiving of presents.
I love it all!

Humbled was I this year by a greater love
and the greatest Christmas gift of all.

Frank Baillargeon - 2014

Come Sit with Me For a Moment

Come. Sit with me for a moment
By this river, ever-flowing.
Share with me these photos of Christmas
    past we shared.

Look at these, so long ago
When our river was breaking free.

A Mom and Dad and their three kids by a
    lovely Christmas tree.

Come. Sit with me for a moment.
We'll take some time to see
How we've journeyed from then to now
    on our river flowing free.

Let's turn this page together
And watch the years march on.

See, we've gone from being kids ourselves
    to seeing you grown and gone.

Come. Sit with me for a moment
My children, if you please,
For it's Christmas past with each of you
    that matters most to me.

The river is ever-flowing.
We've traveled so very far.
These photos mark each Christmas time
    and always touch my heart.

Come. Sit with me for a moment.
My most precious grandchildren.
These old Christmas photos now link you
    all to me.

This river is ever-flowing,
As our journeys carry on.
So, we cherish the times we've shared and
    all those yet to come.

Come. Sit with me this Christmas Eve.
Let's gather, young and old,
To capture one more memory or story to
    be told.

For the river is ever-flowing,
And our journey carries on.

For the river is ever-flowing,
And our journey carries on.

Frank Baillargeon - 2015

An Ode to Christmas of 1967

A boy. A girl. Nineteen-years-old both.
    Freshly married husband and wife.
Enjoying their first Christmas together at
    the start of a long, shared life.
No car quite yet. No lofty dreams.
    Possessions are few, but few required.
Together, they took their first steps
    toward the millions now acquired.

A first Christmas, a child on his way. First
    maternity clothes with so much room
    to spare.
First tree. First ornaments. First cards.
    First presents wrapped with care.
I hold the memories through all these
    years, so distant yet clear.
Heaven had shined down upon me and
    brought me you, my dear.

Now, Christmas number fifty-one is
    somehow here this day.

To count the blessings that we have
        gathered on the way
It would run on far too long to fill an
        eight-by-ten-inch page.
So, let's say the sixty-seven was the year
        that set the stage.

Upon that stage would soon appear our
        children, two and three,
To be thrilled by Santa's visits and the
        presents at the tree.
They trimmed the trees, devoured snacks,
        and lifted voices to heaven.
Those traditions became their own to
        carry on what began in sixty-seven.

Of all the blessings I have known, and
        there have been so many,
I know for sure that without your love,
        there would be hardly any.
The birth of Christ reminds us we are
        called upon to love.
And on this Christmas Day, for you, my
        dear, I thank the stars above.

Frank Baillargeon - 2017

Acknowledgments

I want to thank my family for supporting me through my writing endeavors and inspiring me to put this collection of writings together.

I especially want to thank my wife, Pat, for being my main support and being the first editor to help me critique and polish my works.

One of my objectives when deciding to publish this collection was to have it as enjoyable to look at as it is satisfying and easy to read. That was made possible by the editing skills of Stacey Smekofske of Edits By Stacey, LLC. Thank you.

Finally, I want to thank my granddaughter, Annelise. The cover art for this book was created by Annelise Joy Farquhar, who also created the cover art for my Ambitions series of historical novels. Annelise was awarded an honorable mention for cover art by Bookfest 2023 for volume two of Ambitions, the Life and Love of John and Susannah Morrissey. I am grateful for her willingness to share her talents with me in making these books beautiful.

❄

About the Author

Frank Baillargeon and his wife, Pat, have been married for 56 years. They have lived in Eagle, Idaho, for nearly 25 of those years. For many of their Christmases, Frank prepared and shared a holiday writing to celebrate the holiday season. Some have been poems, some prose, some songs, some serious, some humorous. This volume is an effort to organize a selection of these, publish them, and gift a copy to family and friends. The title, Come Sit with Me for a Moment, represents life as a river journey shared at precious moments with our loved ones.

Frank spent his childhood on Van Schaick Island, where the Hudson and Mohawk Rivers converged at Cohoes, New York. He was educated at Keveny Memorial Academy (class of '66), Hudson Valley Community College (AA '73), and the University of Rochester (BA American History Honors '75).

Frank and Pat welcomed their third and final child during Frank's final year at Rochester. Pat pursued her education at various colleges and universities while juggling parenting, household responsibilities, and caring for other families' children. She graduated with a B.S. (Business Computer Methods) from Long Beach State University (class of '81). Pat explored the high-tech professional world but found her true calling in early childhood development, a business in which she excelled for 30 years.

After retirement, Frank devoted time to fulfilling a commitment to his late father. Using his father's research, Frank published the first two volumes of Ambitions – The Life and Love of John and Susannah Morrissey. Volume Three will be published in mid-2024. Volume two was recently awarded first place in historical fiction by Bookfest's 2023 annual award contest. Annelise Farquhar, the granddaughter of Frank, received an honorable mention from Bookfest for her cover illustration in Volume Two, a well-deserved recognition for her immense talent.

 facebook.com/fjbaillargeon